GOD
DESTINY
CONNECTIONS

A Sequence of Personal Events That Changed the Way I Think and Live

Thomas Livingston Danzey III

ISBN 979-8-89345-399-7 (paperback)
ISBN 979-8-89345-400-0 (digital)

Christian Faith Publishing
832 Park Avenue
Meadville, PA 16335
www.christianfaithpublishing.com

Printed in the United States of America

PREFACE

Prepare to enter my world—a mixture of peculiar parenting, unique siblings, family tragedies, and the mystical revelations that connected them all. Stay with me to the end, and I'll share a glimpse of the hereafter I was privileged to see.

I was born in October 1951 into a lower-middle-class family. I had both a mother and a father as I grew up, which, to me, was a blessing. I had three very different sisters. Looking back, as a family unit, we were very diverse in personalities and how we lived our lives. For the most part, we were a relatively dysfunctional family unit, as will be evident as I proceed. Since the word *dysfunctional* can be interpreted differently based on one's life experience, I will leave it up to you to determine what it means to you. People perceive what is normal based on their experiences associated with their family, community, faith, ethnicity, country, and economic status. *Normal* is a subjective term.

This story recalls events I've lived and sights I've seen, and I'm telling it as truthfully as my mind recalls it.

I've felt a calling to tell this story for quite some time. Despite feeling like a misfit, I realized God has a plan for me. No matter what your situation, hopefully, reading my story will help you recognize that God has a plan for you too.

CHAPTER 1

Dad

My father was an alcoholic, and that made life difficult. We moved at least eight times that I can remember; however, it could have been more since I don't recall my first three years of life. My dad would drink and give away most of his paychecks, and we couldn't pay the rent or utilities. My father had a good heart. He would help people, make them laugh when they needed it, and, most of all, treat people with respect. However, that was when he was sober. His battle with alcohol was a serious challenge for the family. Sober, he was loved by many, but under the influence of alcohol, he was a mean and explosive person. To most older people, I would describe him as a junkyard dog. For those who can't relate to the term *junkyard dog*, I will explain. Owners of junkyards would look for the scariest, meanest dogs to protect the junkyard from trespassers and thieves. They would usually be chained up during the day and released to roam the junkyard at night and attack invaders of the property.

Most of those times, when my dad would get drunk, he couldn't remember the things he had done. One time, I was given the task of finding him. I found him in a bar, and he was about to get into a bar fight. I pulled him out of the bar, and he threw a punch at me, saying I humiliated him. The next day, he didn't remember anything.

Being away from the family most of the time since I was seventeen, I am not sure why and exactly when he decided to stop drinking, but he did. Yes, there were some setbacks, but they were far

1

more the exception than the norm. This change resulted in the most prosperous and respectful years of his life.

He was fun to be with and a very much loved dad. I regret I didn't have that much time to spend with him during those good years. Living away, working, and raising a family put limits on my time.

He developed a high level of economic success. He and my mother traveled the world as part of his work, acquiring many insights relating to life outside the United States. These are things we all should be blessed to experience. As you will see, my connection with my father has been active long after his passing. He passed away a better person than he was for the first fifty years of his life.

Yes, I miss him.

CHAPTER 2

Mom

My mother was bipolar by today's terminology, I believe. *Bipolar* seems to be a catchall term used to describe abnormal behavior that isn't covered by any other diagnosis. She had a fixation with numbers and serious mood swings.

She would spend hours almost every day working on numbers to play in an illegal numbers gambling game, which is similar to the now-legal lottery games. People would pick three numbers based on that day's stock market closing number and put money on their picks. This was played through organized crime at bars.

She believed that numbers weren't random but were part of sequencing in which numbers follow trends. She was pretty successful with her mathematics. She was successful at winning. It always seemed to happen when we most needed it. When she wasn't into the numbers, she would start cleaning with a rage. That is, she would beat that vacuum cleaner to death. It was almost like that vacuum cleaner made her mad.

If you walked into the house while she was in the middle of her vacuum rage, she would start yelling at you because you needed to start cleaning too. After school, I used to look through the window to see what was going on. If it was the vacuum rage, I would go up to the basketball courts and play till dark. I figured I would rather be yelled at for not coming home than dealing with her cleaning rage.

She did her best to keep us together and off the streets. She did not want us to become hoodlums. She believed kids on the streets at night were looking for trouble. She did her best under very tough conditions.

My mom recognized the importance of having a strong belief in faith. She raised us as Catholics and sent us to religious classes.

My mother not only raised me and my sisters but also took in my nephew when his mother died in a car accident and his father was otherwise occupied and not available to raise him.

Looking back, she was a good mother and did what she could under very trying circumstances. I'm not sure if anybody appreciated the daunting tasks she performed to keep this family together. Going forward, you will see some of the tough decisions she had to make.

Sometimes, I cannot believe how she managed everything. Sadly, however, I am of the opinion that the battle to save the family drove her to travel the path of my father, and she became an alcoholic as well. She was a crazy, tough woman and a survivor.

She was Mom—you had to love her.

CHAPTER 3

Cindy

My sister Cindy was one year older than me, a brilliant person, and a significant influence on me. Cindy is like reading two different books. During her earlier years, she and I weren't very close. She was a very intelligent and talented person. I couldn't compete with her in either intelligence or talent.

The sad thing was that she was a year ahead of me in school, and I had to follow her. Teachers seemed to think I was supposed to be on the same intellectual level as my sister. I might have been there, but my level of motivation wasn't up to hers.

Cindy could sing, dance, act, and be academically at the top of her class. On the downside, she was boy crazy, which I believe generated some of the toughest times in her life. Older boys fascinated her.

When she was twelve years old, the older boys were already chasing her. Looking back, I was an enabler by covering for her to my mother. She would be out running with the older boys, and I would tell my mother she was at the library or at some school event.

I was always protective of my sisters, but at that age, I didn't realize the potential downside of my actions. When Cindy was seventeen, working in a drugstore after school, she met a twenty-six-year-old engineer who charmed her. She became infatuated with him and became pregnant. He then ran off.

During that time, Cindy's life became complicated, to say the least. I don't believe she ever contemplated abortion.

I also believe my mother convinced her that wasn't an option and that the family would help her while raising what turned out to be her wonderful son.

Later in life, my mother informed me that she herself had an abortion when she was younger and that she lived each day of her life regretting that decision. Due to that regret, she instilled a strong conviction of the right to life in Cindy and me.

She became angry and was out to punish other men's lives. I guess I can understand that since the feeling of betrayal was fresh and painful. She fell away from the church as I did. I believe the church gave her a hard time about baptizing her son. It hurt her and me. I was his godfather. The church didn't want to baptize him due to his father, but somehow they worked it out. I love that boy and always will. Cindy was strong, and everything she did would eventually find the right path.

Cindy dated a few married men and may have hurt some families. During this time, she met a man who changed the direction of her life, her husband-to-be, Walter. This marriage had its complications at the start, but they figured it out.

She went back to the church and became very successful in everything she touched. She started her own company and was excellent at investing in real estate. During this time, I can say she allowed God back into her life. She was kind, generous, happy, and involved in the church.

Cindy and Walter were married about two weeks prior to my marriage to Alyce. We lived about an hour apart and spent many weekends together. This is when Cindy and I reconnected.

Cindy and I talked about many things in life and were friendly shoulders to cry on. We talked about God and my relationship with the church. Cindy made me smile.

Cindy developed breast cancer in the early 1990s, and she remained strong during her treatment and surgery. I know she prayed hard and talked to God constantly.

Fortunately, she went into remission. She changed her lifestyle and would laugh more and avoid stress. Cindy became my closest confidant, next to my wife. Sometimes success can bring stress into our lives, and it's my belief that that stress showed its head again when her cancer reappeared as it metastasized in her liver. She died in November of 2008. It broke my heart.

CHAPTER 4

Shelia

My second sister, Shelia, was two years younger than me. I affectionately referred to her as Monk because she was small and had long arms like a monkey. She was very close to me. She was my buddy.

If I was being bullied while delivering my papers, without fear, she would jump right in to help me. She was athletic, more so than many of the boys, and would play all sports with me and my friends. She was the brother I never had.

She had her demons, much like my dad's. She was smart and fun until she started drinking. Once the alcohol took control of her, it became her lifetime battle and contributed to her demise.

Shelia started drinking in high school. She would climb out of her bedroom window on the second floor and meet up with her girlfriends. They would drink liquor they stole from their parents' bar.

My father caught her once and covered for her with my mother. I've heard it said that people with alcoholism will cover for each other. I guess it's true.

When she drank, she would say some of the meanest things about people to their faces. She hurt a lot of people and ruined relationships. I will say this, however, she never said a bad thing to me.

I guess that's why it hurt, knowing she would eventually die from this disease. I told her I didn't want to be a part of her suicide.

Her life was not easy by any means. She had a lot of mountains to climb. At one point, she was visiting friends in Florida and was climbing a tree wearing flip-flops just to see the sunrise. She always loved the beautiful things nature would provide.

However, this time her love of the sunrise brought her years of pain and rehabilitation. Her flip-flop got caught in the tree, and she fell to the ground after being beaten by every branch on the way down. She shattered her ear and part of her skull. Even worse, she damaged her spine.

The doctors weren't sure she would ever walk correctly, or even walk at all. That was not acceptable to Shelia. She worked hard—determined to win—and win she did.

After years of hard work and determination, she started running. She ran numerous marathons. She was special.

She passed away in September 2016.

I miss her sense of humor, her expressions, her caring. She loved animals and was one of the best at training them. She would help anyone in need.

Other than her issue with alcohol, she was an awesome person. I still stay connected with her wife, Elise, who helps remind me of how unique she was, yet how wonderful she was.

Shelia nicknamed me Broski. I miss hearing that word. Elise gave my wife, Alyce, and me a little sprout from one of Shelia's plants, and Alyce nicknamed it Broski. In just a few years, it grew five feet tall and will be with me till I pass on.

I hope God, being as great as God is, has taken her, and she has found peace. I'm a Christian, but I can't say that she was. My faith says you must go through Jesus to get to the Father.

With us being mere mortals and limited in our comprehension of what God thinks, I believe God knows a good person, a person of heart, and understands what it means to be human with all our faults and will take her into his arms.

CHAPTER 5

Tina

My youngest sister, Tina, was an unexpected addition to the family. She was almost eight years younger than me. My dad nicknamed her Sam after a character in Dr. Seuss's book, *Green Eggs and Ham*, a favorite of my dad.

I missed most of her life.

During some of the most difficult times for our family, my mother had to make some unbelievably tough decisions. One was to have my aunt take my newborn sister and raise her for a few years.

I left home for college at age seventeen and never really returned. I would visit as I could during the years I was in college and the Navy. I missed most of the years while Tina was growing up. I only lived with her for five years and never really developed a bond like with my other sisters.

Like everyone in my family, she had a rough period in her life. She suffered an abusive first marriage and was divorced. She had two children. Tina was strong and eventually found a good man, and they were married. His name was Tom. I must say I like that name. They have two children of their own. Tina was tall and athletic and could do just about anything, and probably has.

Tina is a survivor; she has a unique ability to do whatever needs to be done in order to move forward. She and her husband, Tom, are as adventurous as any couple you will ever meet. They will do anything as a means to survive. They have probably had more occupations than anyone I know. They are successful at managing to make things work.

Tina will forever be young. I look back and feel bad I wasn't there while she grew up. When I think of her, I see a free spirit, and I'm so proud of her.

We have bonded as we got older. She has a great family and a strong family. I always feel refreshed after seeing them.

CHAPTER 6

Alyce

In August 1974, I met my wife, Alyce. It was a meeting nobody could have predicted. I was in Pittsburgh, she was in Baltimore, and it was a blind date. I had just gotten out of the military in May and was in Pittsburgh trying to figure out what was next in my life. I was working as a laborer.

My friend John had met a girl he really liked while at Wildwood, New Jersey. She lived in Baltimore, and he wanted to go see her. It was in late August, and he asked me to go along with him. At first, I said no. I didn't want to just hang around the two of them.

He said maybe she could set me up with one of her friends. Her friend was younger than me, and I told him I wasn't looking to hang around with a kid.

I was twenty-three. I'd been in college and the military and had already done all the crazy stuff, so I didn't want to hang with kids. John told her that, and she came up with an alternate plan.

She said there was a nice lady who had just started working with her who was from Cleveland, and she believed she might be more my age. That lady was Alyce. John talked me into going.

In my freshman year at Auburn University, I had a blind date with a girl named Alice, and it was a respectful but not enjoyable experience. I can't believe John convinced me to go on another blind date with someone named Alyce.

We got to Baltimore and stayed at the house of the parents of John's girlfriend. They were good people. We went to pick up Alyce to go to a club for talk and music. When Alyce opened the door to her apartment, and I saw her for the first time, I was mesmerized. She was perfect.

We went to the club and talked and danced, and I knew this was someone very special. Think of it as if you finally figured out the meaning of life.

At the end of the evening, we dropped Alyce at her apartment and went back to the house of the parents of John's girlfriend. John and I were leaving in the morning to drive back to Pittsburgh.

Two weeks later, John wanted to go back. I agreed to go, hoping Alyce would like to go out with me again. John's girlfriend said Alyce was interested in seeing me again.

We went to Baltimore, and I went to pick up Alyce, and she was all dressed. I got all upset because I thought she had been out with someone already. My jealous nature showed up, and she didn't understand. She told me she got dressed up because she knew I was coming. I felt like a fool.

The next day, we decided to go to Ocean City, Maryland. Alyce had never been to the ocean. We were walking down the boardwalk, and I looked at Alyce and said, "This may sound crazy, but you and I are going to get married." The look on her face when I said this was one of being stunned.

John and his girlfriend decided we should stay the night rather than drive back to her house. We would be all in the same room. Only two queen-size beds!

Guys weren't going to sleep with guys, so after a long discussion, I told Alyce I would sleep on top of the blanket, and she would sleep under. She agreed, and all was well. I knew then that she was special.

In the morning, John and I dropped the girls off, and we headed back to Pittsburgh. Two weeks later, I made a decision to take care of my affairs in Pittsburgh and move to Baltimore.

It's October, and I'm in Baltimore, staying at the house of the parents of John's girlfriend and looking for a job. I told Alyce I was in town and looking for a job. Alyce would cook meals and have me over.

I got a job in electronics repair, which is what I was trained for in the Navy. On October 31, 1974, I called Alyce during my lunch and asked her if she was ready. She said, "Yes."

I told my boss I would be off the rest of the day; I was getting married. I picked Alyce up from her job, went to the courthouse, and we were married.

How is that for Halloween? Who would believe a woman who went to Catholic schools all her life and graduated from Ohio Dominican College would end up with a person like me?

After about six months of marriage, I told Alyce that I needed to go back to Auburn and finish what I started. I promised if she would agree to do this with me, that when I graduated, I would go wherever she wanted.

She told me okay, but we'd be moving to Cleveland to be with her family. I said okay and that I would never take her away from them unless she wanted to move. The deal was done! Alyce left her job, and we headed to Auburn University.

At Auburn, Alyce took a job waiting on tables. It was hard work, but she never complained. Alyce later took a position working as manager of a large pizza business.

She got me a job there, and I worked with her, flipping pizzas, making sandwiches, and doing some deliveries. We also took on the cleanup of the restaurant. Alyce worked very hard and yet never complained.

I went to school all year around and finished in two years, and yes, we went to Cleveland, Ohio, and have never left.

She was a mother to three beautiful children. I don't think there could be a better mother than she was. She has endured challenges that no one should have to endure.

Alyce was the angel that I needed to help me through life during all the good and bad times. She is the most caring and kind person I have ever known—a great wife, mother, friend, and confidant. I have been blessed that she has stayed with me for forty-nine years, so far. It is no wonder people call her Saint Alyce.

CHAPTER 7

Mary Kate

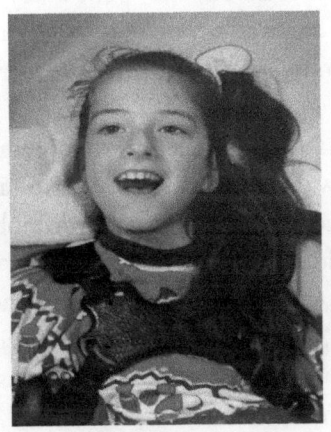

Mary Kate

Mary Kate was born on October 21, 1983. That was the beginning of one of the most stressful and emotional periods of my life. Now I realize the importance of life and the need to fight for it.

Mary Kate was born suffering from RDS (respiratory distress syndrome), a situation where the body was not producing surfactin, which allows her lungs to take in air and let it out without the lungs sticking together. She was born in one hospital and then life-flighted to a neonatal intensive care unit (NICU). There, she was receiving the best care you can get in Cleveland.

Alyce had to remain at the original hospital because of her C-section. I had to leave her to be with Mary Kate.

Alyce was so upset that she signed herself out of the hospital wearing this large protective wrap around her incision area and had her sister drive her to the other hospital.

The original hospital called her doctor and told him what she did. He then contacted the second hospital to have an emergency crew ready for her.

Mary Kate was placed in the NICU. I kept remembering what the doctor told me when Tommy was born about touching the baby. I spent that night and every night for three months with my hand in the incubator, gently rubbing the hair on her head and talking to her.

When Alyce was released, she spent every day with her. I was working the second shift and would go right to the hospital after work. Alyce would come every morning. We were told the odds were against her.

In the NICU, I remember seeing what seemed like one hundred babies, and nobody was there for them. During my time there, I saw probably twenty babies die, and yet there was nobody there for them.

The doctors told us that if Mary Kate survived, she would be handicapped due to the levels of oxygen she had received. We told them we understood, but we wanted her to survive.

We were asked if we had other children as if that would be a determining factor in our decision.

I try to have faith in mankind, but it's hard when people aren't trying to be there for their own flesh and blood.

Mary Kate made it home three months later, thank God. She influenced everybody she came in contact with, especially her siblings and all the extended family on Alyce's side and mine.

Even the family dogs, in particular, my sister's dog Timba, recognized her as special. I would lay Mary Kate on the couch, and she would laugh and swing her arms at seeing Timba, who was a very large white German shepherd. Timba would kiss her and lay by her in a protective posture. It put tears in my eyes.

We were told that Mary Kate would probably only live six years, at best. I'm here to tell you that unconditional love can alter the odds.

She lived nineteen wonderful years, and her smile and waving hands changed many a life.

She would be there in her wheelchair, waiting for me to come home. When I came into the house, she would light up like the Fourth of July. I would take her out of her wheelchair and hold her, and she would smile at me like I was the greatest.

I always say she took the beast of anger out of me. If I was angry, she would look at me and cry. It would break my heart, and I would just hold her.

When I would change her diaper and her trach, she would just look at me with adoring eyes, and I would put on music and dance with her. Those are blessed moments. She had some tough medical times and times that challenged my faith, but she always came back smiling. True love is hard to lose without questioning God. Everybody who met her treated her with kindness and understood the meaning of unconditional love.

Alyce took care of Mary Kate with the kindness of an angel. This is no surprise, as Mary Kate was an angel and had an angel care for her. Alyce was amazing, and I loved Mary Kate so much that I asked myself, *Why has God blessed me with such a beautiful person?*

CHAPTER 8

Tommy

Tom and Alecia

Tommy is my son. He was born in August 1978, ten weeks premature. It was a scary and emotional time. After a long and hard labor, Alyce ended up having a cesarean section. I remember the doctor telling me to touch Tommy when he was put in the incubator. He said that touch would be important in his chances of surviving. Survive he did. He became the biggest eater in the nursery, all five pounds and two ounces of him. He was a beautiful baby.

Growing up, Tommy was an average student in school and loved sports. He was never a problem, and as unbelievable as that sounds, it's totally true. He never questioned my authority. One time, I asked why it was that he never challenged me, saying, "No."

His response was a simple: "That's okay. I'll just deal with it."

He loved his mother. Everything she did was the greatest. She would make him a meal, and he would say it was the best ever. Tommy and Alyce had a very special bond. Tommy's bond with me was very different. I was hard on him. I taught him to be a man like my father taught me. We don't cry, we're strong, and we project that image. This was a mistake. However, he was smarter than I thought. He listened and developed his own personality.

Tommy loved the weight room and football. He liked hard work. We used to wrestle and play what I called The Tiger and the Cub, but eventually, he grew out of the cub stage and became another tiger. Two large men wrestling and breaking the couch into two pieces was a lesson. Alyce put an end to the macho stuff. He had become too strong for me to handle.

He would play with all the little kids in the family and never hurt them. He was especially attached to Mary Kate. I loved seeing this big powerful young man be so tender with her. He would play with her and make her feel like everyone else. He would pile up all the cushions and pillows from the couch and let her roll into the pillows from our bed. She would laugh and wave her hands with excitement. She loved him dearly.

Tom would come home from college to babysit her, just so Alyce and I could go see Alecia play basketball in college. I remember coming home, and we would see all the pillows and cushions all over the room. And there would be Tommy and Mary Kate, sleeping together on the floor—side by side. This was heartwarming, for sure. He would always check on her when we were at family events. They had a special bond.

Alecia, our second child, and Tommy had a different bond. I believe they would laugh about me most of the time. They were both athletes, competitive, but caring. I would say Tommy was loved by the whole family, both immediate and extended. His cousins said he was quite the storyteller. The stories were usually about his crazy father.

CHAPTER 9

Alecia

Alecia was our first daughter. From the moment she was born, we knew she was something special. She always had a free spirit. Alyce and I would lie in bed and laugh, listening to her scream, "Mom!" demanding we get her out of the crib.

Alecia was a good student, athlete, and person. She was a strong-minded girl, which was good for this generation. She could play any sport she chose and be good at it. She made many friends, and those friendships have lasted forever.

Alecia was much like her brother in that she always kept an eye on Mary Kate. She would always give her attention, and she would pass by her and make sure she was okay. Alyce's father told me how proud he was of Alecia and Tommy because they never go by Mary Kate without giving her attention.

Alecia spent most of her school years and summers playing organized sports. When she wasn't practicing, she was at games. She had good grades and never gave us any trouble.

She definitely would challenge my decision-making. That was fine by me. I wanted her to be strong and challenge what she thought was wrong. She also stood up for her big brother. I remember her yelling at me and hitting me because she thought I was being too hard on Tommy. She wanted me to back off.

Funny, at that moment, I got this warm feeling and smiled. I realized she was doing just what I would want from her, sticking up for her brother.

I remember at one of her soccer games, I was too loud with the referees, so she made me sit up on the hill, about seventy-five yards away, so I could yell into the wind. The girl has spunk!

Alecia and Alyce have a bond that's stronger than love itself. It warms my heart! They are always in contact. It's a bond a father would be jealous of, but not me. I realize that their relationship is exactly what I would want it to be.

Alecia went to college, graduated in four years, then went forward and added an accelerated nursing program, and received a BS degree in nursing. Later, she completed her master's degree.

Alecia married a good man, Chad, and they have two children. She is a wonderful person and mother. She works extremely hard. I'm very proud of her, and yes, she still challenges me!

CHAPTER 10

Who Am I

I prefer this writing not to become my biography, but you need to know a bit about me to put everything into context. I am human, complete with all the complexity, frailty, courage, pettiness, and hopes that come with it. Being human, there were certain events in my life, parts where I probably have emotionally hurt people. I need not detail these events because they may needlessly open wounds for those I hurt.

I am no angel or a saint. I am just a man. I stressed this to my children so they wouldn't put me on a pedestal as something I am not. I have spent half my life trying to be a better person than I was the day before.

As I travel through my life, I try not to repeat the mistakes I have made. I wish in some cases I could go back in time and make better decisions. However, that is not possible, so all I can do is learn from them and try not to repeat them.

During my preteen years, I was pretty much a quiet kid. These were formative years when I spent time putting my thoughts together and trying to make sense of all the events and my reactions to those events. Trying to decide what is normal and what's not.

As a child, we all have experiences that are hard to label as normal since they are usually first-time experiences, and we don't know if everyone goes through the same things. Some of those experiences are uncomfortable, and you feel you can't talk about them, especially if you think that they may be abnormal. Even as I look back today, I am not sure of the answer to some of those experiences.

Growing up from childhood to entering puberty and making it through college were interesting challenges. I thought a lot about all the things going on in my life and my family. I looked at life as a book, in which there are some parts I liked and some I didn't.

I would promise myself that I would change those things I didn't like and keep those I thought were good. Easily said, but hard to do! Sometimes things seem to be genetically inherited from family history and are hard to understand. During my formative years, there were events that have stayed implanted in my brain as being significant. Let's begin at the age when I truly started remembering things.

I was three years old, and we were living in Trenton, New Jersey. We lived in a row house in a community of row houses. There was my sister Cindy, baby Shelia, and myself. One day, we were put to bed for the night; we all slept in one big bed. Shelia was asleep, and Cindy and I were looking out the window. I thought it was so unfair we had to go to bed while it was lights-out and other kids were playing. I don't know why, but this feeling of things being unfair became a vivid memory for me, and the emotions tied to it are still as real today when I feel something is unfair.

I remember seeing my dad drunk and falling while he was yelling and screaming. It didn't register as not being normal at that time. My mother would always sweep us away to the bedroom to hide what was going on. Then there was the time my mother took us to a neighbor's house, where I watched four policemen fighting with my dad as they placed him in a police car. The violence was extreme by both my dad and the police. This was the first time I felt the pain of loving. I cried and hurt so deeply that it hurts me still today when looking back at it.

I remember my first feeling of fear. My mother and I left the row house to go to the store. We got to the store, and after my mother got what she came for, we left. The wind had picked up and felt very strong to me. I realized it looked like my mother had walked far away from me. I was so scared I was going to be left behind, and I didn't know where our house was. To this day, I relive that fear when remembering that day.

It's funny how much that day influenced my feelings as it pertains to children. I hate fear and the paralyzing effect it has. Nothing bothers me more than seeing a child in fear. The fear I felt on that day has permeated my dreams ever since we had our own children, as you will soon see.

It is funny how some events can become memories that trigger a response years down the road that are unrelated. When we were evacuating Trenton because of a hurricane, I remember seeing all the signs, lights, and wires striking the road and thinking how awesome that was. To this day, there are unrelated songs that take me back to that night and make me smile.

The only other thing I remember from Trenton was learning to ride a two-wheel bike. The bike was a standard twenty-four-inch-high bike. I had to stand on the steps to get on and off.

We moved from Trenton to the country just outside of Pittsburgh, Pennsylvania, to Clinton, Pennsylvania, in 1957. This was my paternal grandparents' house. It was there I realized how much I loved being in the country with open spaces and nature.

It was also at this point that I realized that my father had a serious problem. He lost his car, probably as the result of repossession, but that didn't stop him from finding his way to the bar. My dad would drive his father's riding lawn mower through the back roads and down the highway a couple of miles just to go drink. The bar my dad patronized was always in trouble because of shootings and knife fights.

I went to Independence School for first grade, and I have a few interesting memories of it. First, I developed a crush on my teacher. She was pretty and nice and made me feel warm. Second, I remember I was afraid to go to the bathroom at school because of rumors that the sixth graders would put people's heads in the toilet. Needless to say, I was in distress after school.

Going to school, we walked through a country community down Backbone Road, a gravel road, and then across a bridge over the creek to catch the school bus. Going home was the opposite, and every day, I never got past the bridge without taking care of my bathroom problems.

Third, our school served lunch and would give sweet pickles with our hamburgers. Nobody liked them but me. Everybody gave them to me, and I ate them, and then I got sick on the bus. Again, I left something at the bridge. To this day, I won't eat sweet pickles.

Lastly, during recess at school, the kids played games at the playground. I would collect bugs instead. I remember it was a nice day, and I had a big paper bag of bugs I collected and put it in my desk. This was a lift-up top type desk. My desk wouldn't completely close due to how I stacked my books. The class went to lunch, and when we came back, the room was covered with bugs. It wasn't intentional, but I was punished. I guess my teacher didn't feel the same about me as I did her!

Our stay in Clinton wasn't that long. I assumed it was because my grandparents were coming back home or because my mom and dad separated. I didn't understand this process at that time.

My mom took us kids and went to stay at the house of my mother's father in Carnegie, Pennsylvania. My mother's father had passed, and his home seemed a sanctuary home for family members who were in need of a place to stay for whatever reason. Think about it: two single adults and two families minus the husbands living under one roof, with only three bedrooms. I can't say how long we stayed there, but I went through third grade there at St. Luke Catholic School.

There were two major memories from that time frame that I remember: first, the nuns, and second, seeing my father for the first time since my parents' separation. The nuns, I believe, didn't like me. They seemed to always find a reason to punish me.

For example, if I didn't have my bow tie clipped on while outside playing during recess, I was punished. There was another time when, after being bullied by some older kid who threw a stone at me, I then picked up a piece of slate and threw it at him, but it stuck in his leg. They punished me but not him. Seemed unfair!

The biggest incident, as I look back at it now, is kind of funny, but not to an eight-year-old. My mother sent my younger sister Shelia and me to go to church on Sunday. We walked to the church at St. Luke's School. We were early, and another kid was also there. I just happened to have a pocket full of baseball cards in my pocket. The other boy had cards too. As boys would do back then, we started gambling on the steps leading into the church by flipping cards. I won all his cards.

Doors opened, and we went into the church and sat in a pew, the three of us. The other boy and Shelia were laughing and talking during mass. Unknown to me, they would pull people's shoes off when they kneeled. People were mad, and so were the nuns who were sitting behind us on the balcony. Needless to say, they blamed me! I got the standard punishment from the principal, plus I had to write a letter to the bishop. The nuns seem to see everything!

It's funny when you go to school, they tell you the right thing to do, which is to come forth and tell the truth. Then they punish the hell out of you.

I was the Beaver Cleaver in our class. Every morning, we would have time where we got in line to take care of any business we had with the teacher. I decided to get in line, do the right thing, and tell the teacher I didn't do my homework. Bad decision—public embarrassment, punishment, and a call to my mother followed. Lesson learned.

This second memory has stuck with me and will go to the grave with me. For some reason, probably for us kids' sake, my mother took us to see my dad. This would be the first time in at least six months or more that I would see him. We met on the sidewalk, and all I could remember was the terrible hurt I felt, and I broke down and cried harder than I can ever remember at that time. I wanted to be with my dad so much. I never wanted to let go when my mom was pulling me away to go back to my grandfather's house. Even today, when I hear of children being separated from one parent, it tears at me. I don't know if this was the catalyst for them getting back together, but shortly thereafter, it happened.

Well, needless to say, my parents got a place in Greentree, Pennsylvania, for us to live together. It was a house that they rented. Things didn't last too long, and we relocated to a rental in Crafton,

Pennsylvania, which wound up being a three-year stay. Not that things were different, but assistance from my aunt Anastasia, my mom's sister, saved us from more moves.

This was a very tough time, even though my sisters and I had some semblance of a normal life. We made good friends at one school. However, things were still the same at times, for example, not having electricity or regular food. My aunt Anastasia, God bless her, provided money to keep us going.

The worst thing that a child can imagine occurred. My mother gave my little sister Tina to my aunt Anastasia and her husband, Mike, to raise till whenever she and my dad got things right. Not only was I gone from Tina's growing up since she was nine years old, but also at least her first four years. My dad was still the same. I give my mom a lot of credit for trying to make it work.

During this time period, the bullying against me stopped. I learned how to fight. I found I had a bad temper, which my mother swore she would beat out of me. You can imagine how well that worked.

I also learned about the facts of life earlier than I needed and thought I was in love with most girls I met. Three years went by, and we moved again. This time, we moved to Wilkinsburg, on the other side of Pittsburgh. We were there for another three years.

Wilkinsburg introduced me to an integrated school. This was the first time I associated with black students. The fact is, I had a better relationship with the black students than the white ones. I was smaller in stature, still looked like Beaver Cleaver, and still had my temper. I had a problem with one of the white gangs after an incident. But I learned to run, to hide in a crowd, and escape through buildings. It was all a learning process.

I grew ten inches between the end of eighth grade and the beginning of ninth grade. Then the problems stopped. It seems it always took a show of strength to get peace.

For most of these three years, I spent most of the time covering for my boy crazy sister, Cindy, with my mom. My dad was improving. He became more involved with us kids. He had to take jobs sometimes out of state, but he was always happy to come home. I truly believe he missed us.

I think he worked hard at trying to quit his drinking. For the most part, I don't remember seeing him drunk then, but I'm sure he probably fell off the wagon a few times.

I was blessed to see another side of my dad that I loved. He would take me and my sisters to all the football games. He would let us paint the car with our school colors and put streamers on it and then drive us through town while we would scream and cheer, "We are the Tigers—the mighty, mighty Tigers!" This memory warms my heart just thinking about it.

Probably the best thing that happened was when Tina came back to the family. This was very hard for my aunt and uncle. My aunt couldn't have kids.

Then my family moved again. This time to a home they bought. My dad won some money playing the numbers. This was illegal but was basically the same as today's lotto. He won enough for a down payment on a nice home in Penn Hills.

Life at Penn Hills was pretty good except for some family issues, but we all survived them. Besides dealing with family issues, I felt I was a pretty normal kid. I left home at the age of seventeen to enter college. I wanted to be away from home and was accepted to Auburn University in the Deep South. Being the first in the family to leave for college, I was on my own to figure it out.

On my first day in school, I learned three important things that would be with me for two years: first, how to smoke; second, how to drink beer; and third, how deadly sick you could get doing these things. Over the first two years, I met and dated a number of girls and at least two whom I cared deeply about. I found out that I had a terrible jealous streak and that I was very possessive. These two traits are a disaster in relationships.

I was immature with an unbelievable temper, but I never in my life ever hit a woman. Being raised with a mother and three sisters, my dad would have beaten me to within an inch of my life. I under-stood the ramifications of any action of that nature.

I found that my words were just as mean, though. I am not proud of the way I handled myself. I spent a lot of time hurting those that I cared most about. I was a jackass. When you play people and emotionally hurt them, you are not a good person. I was very immature at that time in my life.

Academically, I did pretty well through two-plus years, and then I went and scheduled a nightmare in the third semester—eight in the morning till eight at night—five days with all heavy sciences and labs. I was burnt out!

I quit going to class, didn't take any exams, skipped finals, and left school. Auburn notified the draft board, and the next phase of my life started. I spent 1972 to May 1974 in the Navy.

During my time in the Navy, I met a wonderful girl and got engaged. She was going to college. I visited her, and she was great, but for some reason, it didn't work out. She had a friend, and when she and that guy looked at each other, I saw a glow in their eyes that told me they had feelings. They may not have agreed with me, but I felt it. I broke off the engagement. I never wanted to hurt her. She was special.

While in the Navy, I developed some really bad ankles. They sent me to a naval hospital ship for an examination. The doctor asked me how I got into the military, and I said, "The draft." He then proceeded to tell me I should never have been allowed in; my feet were so bad that they shouldn't have accepted me. He offered me permanent shore duty, or I could leave. Vietnam was winding down, and they were bringing home large numbers of troops, so I got out. I left on May 4, 1974. On October 31, 1974, I married Alyce.

Alyce and I went back to Auburn University in 1975 and used my GI bill to return to school. I graduated in August 1977, and we went to Cleveland, where her family lived. I got a job working for General Motors Corporation.

In 1978, we bought a house, the same one we live in today. We had our son, Tommy, my namesake, in August 1978. In 1979, we had our daughter Alecia. We then had our daughter Mary Kate in October 1981.

Alyce was and still is a sweet person, always looking for the good in people. She is a wonderful and caring mother. She cared for our totally handicapped daughter at home with loving care, not something everyone could handle. She took care of most of the raising of our other two children while I worked.

She was and is a special wife, working hard to keep me balanced and never giving up on me in my darkest moments. I thank God for this angel, and I know that at times, I gave her good reason to be done with me. I don't deserve her, but I believe God sent her my way for a reason. I haven't always made her journey pleasant, and again, some of my actions tend to hurt the people I care about the most. To those I hurt, I'm sorry; I wish I could turn back time.

Overall, I did some bad things in my life. I treated some people so poorly, it haunts me. I used bad judgment and hurt people. Some things I have been forgiven for and some not. I understand that. I have tried to learn from my mistakes and be a better person every day.

CHAPTER 11

The Story

It was Friday, June 25, 1999, and I had just completed a long day's work. I came home looking forward to relaxing. Tommy was at work and wasn't home yet. He liked hard work detailing boats and yachts and worked long hours. He showed up around 6:30 p.m. after ten long hours, took a shower, got dressed, and grabbed a quick bite to eat.

We talked for a few minutes, and he said he was going to his cousin's house. I said okay, and he left.

Saturday morning, around eleven, Tommy woke up and said he was going to the gym and then out with his friends. I said to him that he hadn't gotten much sleep and maybe he needed to slow down. I knew he hadn't come home until after four in the morning.

We were standing in the dining room, and I casually started to talk about his future. He had to leave school as a result of an illness and wasn't available to take his finals. He failed to make up his final due to hospitalization and recovery time.

I asked him what he wanted to do with his future, and he said he didn't know. I told him that I loved him and it would be alright. Tommy looked at me and had a tear on his cheek as he left.

Sunday morning, Tommy was not home. Alyce was at work at the Country Club. I heard a knock at the door, and it was a state patrolman. Not a good feeling.

I answered the door and asked him what he wanted. He informed me that my son was in a car accident and was taken to Southwest Hospital.

I responded, "Is he okay?"

He said, "You need to go to the hospital."

I asked, "Is he dead?" and the officer did not answer. I asked if anyone else was injured, and he said no one else was involved.

I called my wife and told her Tommy was in an accident and that we needed to go to the hospital. Alyce was only about two miles away and drove herself home. Needless to say, she was an emotional train wreck. We weren't in any condition to drive to the hospital.

We reached out to Maureen and Doug, Alyce's sister and her husband who lived nearby. Maureen stayed with Mary Kate, and Doug drove us to the hospital.

We got to the hospital and were told he had passed prior to being brought in. I had never felt such hurt in my life. Alyce was totally immersed in tears, and I didn't know what to say to her.

I was always brought up to be strong in a crisis—to care for my family's pain. We just held each other. You feel so alone. There's no cry for help—nothing can change the outcome. You feel desperate. You don't know what to do. You become numb—you can't believe this is real.

Doug drove us back home. I remember that ride, but my mind was not in a good place. I pride myself on knowing what to do, but I was in a vacuum.

We got home and looked at Mary Kate and thought, *How can I tell her the big boy she loved wouldn't be coming home anymore?* She could see the pain in our faces.

The next thing we had to do was to tell Alecia. Alecia was visiting her boyfriend's family in Findlay, Ohio. Doug said he would take us. Danny, Alyce's brother, came along to bring Alecia's car home.

Alyce called and talked to the mother of my daughter's boyfriend to let her know we were coming but said not to mention anything. Alecia had no idea what she was about to hear.

We got there, I went into the house, and she was waiting. I had no idea how I was going to tell her something that I knew would hurt her so badly. She could see by my face this was bad. She asked, "What's wrong—did Katie die?"

I said, "No, Tommy."

She screamed, called me a liar, and started punching me. I just stood there. I could feel her pain. I just held her. There was nothing I could say.

We left the house, and she got into the car and left with us. I was so lost, I don't remember any conversation we had during the trip home.

When we arrived home, I felt this couldn't be real—this was a mistake. I was tormented with the idea that I somehow let the family down. It has always been my job to keep my family safe. I wanted to take their pain away, but I couldn't. I knew our lives would be forever changed. I realized that now I have to be strong for my wife and daughters.

I can honestly say I don't remember much of the next few days my family was hurting. What I do remember were the nights lying by my wife as she cried herself to sleep. There is nothing more painful than to watch your family hurt, knowing there is nothing you can do to ease their sorrow.

I started feeling guilty and believed that God was doing this because of my sins. I couldn't believe God would bring such pain to the rest of my family because of me. I started to pray harder than I ever had. I prayed not for myself but for my family to find peace. I accepted God's will for myself.

Things had to be done, as is always the case when someone dies. I had no experience in these matters, but everybody in my wife's family jumped in to help make all the arrangements that were necessary. My wife was devastated, my daughter in pain. I knew I had to be strong. I still have my two daughters and my wife, who have to go on living. Mary Kate had a good sense of when something had gone wrong. Who knows, maybe she knew more than all of us. She was very close with Tommy. She would always light up when she saw him.

The wake was huge. Tommy had many great friends. Parents really liked him; he was a good kid. The lines were so long that Alyce and I had to split up to keep the lines moving. It helped to see the outpouring of people and realize how loved he was.

Greeting all those people kept our minds from our sorrow, except when some of them fell apart, reminding us why we were there. We had a closed casket because of the severity of his injuries. It was the right thing to do.

The next day, after the wake, was a mass followed by the burial. The mass was the hardest thing I have ever been through, and it is burnt into my memory like nothing else. The pallbearers were football players, some cousins, and friends of my son, and they were all crying as they brought him down the aisle. I will carry that with me forever.

That was the day, the day when you come face-to-face with the reality that this isn't a dream. The coffin that seals the end of life in this world is being set to rest. My wife and daughter are standing by the site where the coffin is placed, and the final words are spoken. It was a calm day.

As we stood before the crowd of friends, family, and acquaintances to witness this final chapter, a robust, swirling wind surrounded us. This was not just the wind; it was like a living thing moving through the crowd. At this moment, I felt the presence of my son. The wind that was swirling around entered my body like a solid mass and then exited. I could feel him just for that moment, and I felt some peace. It was like I got to hug him, something I didn't do enough while he was alive.

I thought, *Am I crazy or imagining this because of my grief?* This question will be answered later.

It's funny; Tommy's friends picked the music that was playing as we placed dirt on the coffin. That song was "See You on the Other Side" by Ozzy Osbourne. How appropriate is the song, and what can I say, Ozzy?

After the burial, my sister Cindy came over and asked if I felt the wind, and she described it just as I did. She told me she felt him pass through her too.

Cindy was my spiritual partner. We discussed many things, just the two of us. We seemed to be, as they say, "on the same wavelength."

Later, I would come to find out the same thing happened to a few more people who were very close to me or my son. Other people were saying that it was strange how the wind just picked up and then left. Little did I know that this was just a preview of things to come. The hard part now was to figure out how to go forward.

Alyce and I grew closer than ever before. We prayed a lot. In order to keep my mind occupied, I returned to work to force myself from getting lost in the dark hole in my heart.

Moving forward was hard. The nights were filled with tears, and the days were filled with moments of despair. Alyce was strong for a mother losing her firstborn and only son, who admired her, and her him.

Alyce realized she still had her daughters to care for, especially Mary Kate, with all her special needs. Alecia was more independent and carried her grief close to herself. Mary Kate loved her brother. I would show her his picture, and she would light up like a Christmas tree. I knew things were going to be tough.

Shortly after Tom's passing, I started seeing my father's reflection in mirrors and glass panes throughout the house. My father passed away years before Tommy died. When I would shave, he would be staring at me. He would be staring at me when I looked into the big mirror in the family room and the glass panels in the entertainment center.

I told Alyce about this and asked her if I was looking more like my father. My grandfather, my father, my son, and I all carry the same name. My grandfather was the Senior, my dad was the Junior, I was the Third, and my son the Fourth.

After my father died, my sister Shelia, who was so much like my dad, had an encounter with him while driving to work one day. It was icy, and she was coming upon a hill, and she looked over, and he was sitting next to her. He strongly told her to pull over at the top of the hill, and she did, and he was gone. She looked down the hill, and there was a large multicar pileup. Thank God she pulled over.

Looking back, my father, in the late 1950s, was involved in an icy accident when he came over a hill and slid into a doughnut shop, killing a lady. He lived with that all his life.

Coincidence, I didn't know. The women in my family on the Ukrainian side all had visions at times, my sisters included. They were in some way connected to things I couldn't explain.

I was a science and math kind of guy, and I never had any such visions or dreams. I thought they were crazy old-world mumbo jumbo types; after all, I am named Thomas. I understand doubting Thomas. Little did I know how things would change in my future.

The next few months were like nothing one could imagine. I never cried. However, I would spend time every day staring into a dark pit of despair.

I went back to work right away, knowing that if I didn't occupy my mind, I would enter a dark place and not come back. Almost every day, when I allowed myself to focus on my grief, the world around me would disappear, and the vision in my mind would be me in a cave on a ledge looking into a dark pit. I refer to this as the pit of despair.

I would look into it and feel the tremendous sorrow, and it would act like a magnet, trying to pull me in. I knew that if I gave in, I would not come back from this darkness. I would slap my face to wake me from this place of darkness. This was a regular occurrence.

I could be in my office or looking at my computer or watching television. It didn't seem to matter; my vision would focus down like a tunnel, and I would always be standing at the edge of this pit. I would pray, pray like never before to know that my son was okay, and take away this feeling of despair.

During this period, I would stay in contact with my sister Cindy. She was very religious and active in her faith. My mother, sisters, and I were all baptized as Catholics, received our First Communion, and had Confirmation. My sister Cindy and I, for a number of years, strayed from our faith but found our way home again. Cindy got into the church wholeheartedly while I fought in my mind with the church, but was strong with the faith.

I would call her and talk for hours during this time period after Tom's passing. I would call her, and she would call me. As I noted, I was connected with her. It seemed that when I was in my darkest moments, she would call and help keep me afloat.

One day, she called me, and she seemed very serious and said she was working in the yard, and the wind kicked up, and she felt Tommy again, just as it happened at Tommy's gravesite. Little did she know how badly I was feeling at that time. I might say she gave me strength when I needed it.

Trying to be so strong, I would bury my emotions over the loss of Tommy. That would come to an end the day I went to buy our Christmas tree, the first Christmas since Tommy passed. I had been buying my trees from the same place for a few years. The person who helped me get my tree was named Matt. He always seemed to be a good person.

That day, Matt brought my tree to the van and helped me put it on top of the van. Matt then handed me a Christmas wreath for my son's grave. I couldn't speak. I went straight home, went into the bathroom, sat down, and cried as hard as one could cry.

I was raised that men don't cry. We have to be strong for the family. I don't remember the last time I cried. I cried for an hour. I couldn't stop. When I stopped, I felt a tremendous relief, and for the first time in five months, I slept.

After that day, when I was alone, I would still cry, but I needed it. Tears bring temporary relief from the feeling of despair. I can't say why, but it's like taking pain medication for a headache; it gets you through the moment and gives you temporary relief, but the pain comes back. I believe despair is a tremendous feeling of one's inability to cope with the things in your life that you can't change.

You can't change the outcome, and there are no answers. I guess my protective nature causes me to always want to know what I could have done to prevent this outcome, but all this does is make me feel responsible for all the sorrow.

Loss is silence, darkness, and a sense of loneliness. If you allow yourself to be consumed by this feeling and give in to it, you will be lost forever. Nothing good can come from approaching the pit of despair. It is a struggle.

A year later, I still struggled, wanting to know how Tom was doing. I'd have dreams that he was lost and I was looking for him. I'd search and search in my dreams but couldn't find him. By nature, I am a very protective person with my family. I struggle with not fulfilling my duty as a father, and these dreams would tear at me.

The months of June and July were especially rough on me. After many prayers, I had a dream. In this dream, I'm in a church, sitting in the front row praying and still distressed from the battery of dreams of not finding my son. An usher came up to me and said, "You are looking for Tommy, and I want you to know he is here. He's in the back on the patio, eating with your mother-in-law."

I got up and ran to the back of the church, and through the window, I saw a young Tommy sitting with my wife's mother, who had passed away in the early 1990s. At that point, he looked at me, ran into the church, jumped on me, and gave me a hug.

At that point, I woke up, and all that stress went away, and I felt relief and happiness. At this point, my prayers went from "Is he okay?" to "God, talk to me."

In September, I was praying hard, asking God to talk to me. Cindy knew I was under a heavy burden and gave me a call. I told her I'd been praying for God to talk to me, and she said she had also asked God to talk to me. I thanked her for her prayers and updated her on my dreams and other things.

A week had passed since talking to my sister, and I had another dream. In this dream, my sister Cindy came to me and asked me to go with her to church. I agreed to go. She was taking me to a church I didn't recognize. It kind of looked like a Quonset hut. I went into the side door, and she was gone. I looked, and there were all these priests standing in full vestments while a black priest was performing what looked like a blessing of their throats.

Straight down from them was a man who looked just like Jesus in the Sacred Heart picture by my door at home. I began to wonder, *Where has my sister taken me?*

The man was sitting cross-legged on a semicircular bed with scrolls in his lap. As I looked at him, I saw my daughter Mary Kate lying by him in all white, and when she saw me, she started smiling and swinging her arms with excitement.

I said to myself, *What is she doing here?*

I then looked to the right, and there was Cindy, as a little girl, jumping rope in an all-white Communion dress with curls in her hair. I thought to myself, *She is a little girl!* At that moment, I felt a hand on my left shoulder, and I looked—it was Tommy, and he said, "I like it here."

The next thing I knew, the man who looked like Jesus was standing next to Tommy, showing him the scrolls, which had what I would assume to be Hebrew writing on them. Then the man looked at me and, without speaking, said, "I want to talk to you." At this point, I knew it was Jesus.

He walked me to a door, and we stepped out; he spread his arms, hands palm up, and showed me a beautiful green forest with a river flowing through, a beautiful blue sky, and a glass church in the woods.

I turned back, but he was gone, and I woke up. This dream will be significant in my journey, as you will see as the story goes forward. Peace had been found.

It is now January, and I have a new dream. This dream is set in the woods, maybe the beautiful woods of my prior dream. I'm standing with what I know are two angels. There are two men in black leather coats, and there is a little person dressed in a baggy, almost burlap dress with a hood. She is standing on a tree stump, and I am whimpering. The angels are telling me she needs to go with them; she is going to a better place. I go up to her, and she seems old and very thin. I hugged her and told her she needed to go with them.

As they walked away with her, one angel on each side, I looked to the side and yelled, "When did this happen?"

I got a delayed response, which said, "March."

I woke up. I immediately called Cindy and told her about my dream. I believed my sister Shelia was going to die. She'd been sick from her alcoholism and was very skinny, fragile, and old-looking. Cindy listened but didn't respond.

February came along, and the psychic medium John Edward was appearing at Cleveland State University. I convinced Alyce to go with me and see what might happen. Desperate people will do crazy things sometimes to try and get answers.

I am a good-sized fellow, so I put on a bright yellow wind-breaker, hoping to draw his attention. We went and took our seats. John Edward started walking around looking for a connection. He stopped in front of me, and we stared into each other's eyes for about fifteen seconds. After that time, he broke his stare and just looked at me, lowered his head toward the floor, and walked away. I told my wife I thought we were there. Guess I was wrong.

Now it's March, actually the last week of March, and I called Cindy to say I guess I was wrong. I told her this was not a normal dream.

It's March 29, 2001. Alyce is at home with Mary Kate, taking care of her. I was at work, and I got a call from a sobbing Alyce telling me that Mary Kate had died and the rescue department had taken her to the hospital. I left work and went to the hospital. There, I got to hold her one last time. She was an angel loved by all who knew her.

She tamed the beast in me. When I was angry, she would break down crying, and I would take her and hold her because she should never have to cry. She was pure love. My wife, Alyce, is one of the sweetest human beings I know. She kept Katie immaculate. Alyce should never have had to bear all this sorrow.

I called my sister Cindy and then my sister Tina. Tina screamed when I told her and said that she was talking to her daughter Tasha, who was in Mississippi. Tasha told Tina that she woke up, and Kala (Tasha's daughter) was singing "Happy Birthday, Papa."

Tasha asked her, "You mean my dad?"

She said, "No, Papa!" She was referring to my father, whom she never met. Kala said, "He's there," pointing to the corner. She said, "It's Papa's birthday, but the angels are crying today."

Arrangements for Mary Kate's funeral were made, and Alyce and I were trying to decide whether to have an open casket or closed. I told her I would look and see how she appeared after we had agreed to donate her eyes, tissue, and heart valve.

I opened the casket, looked in, and started hyperventilating. It was the girl in my dream. Her skin was pulled and drawn up; her eyes were sunken, and she looked so old, even though she was nineteen. I sat down and got control of myself, and a warm feeling came over me. I told Alyce it would be all right now. I know there is life after here.

Nobody can see the future, but I was given my dream to let me know this was coming so I would recognize there truly is another life. From this point forward, I knew that God is real and there is a purpose for him to want me to have this experience. I don't know what it is, but whatever it is will come to be.

After my experience with Mary Kate, I felt so bad for Alyce because she is such a fine person, a great wife, and a mother; she deserved to be the one having this revelation. Alyce grieves quietly and to herself. She can't talk about these things, and I am like an open book.

For nineteen years, we had lived separate lives in that most of the time, one of us stayed with Mary Kate while the other visited with family. My daughter, Alecia, played college basketball, and my wife didn't get to travel to her games because she didn't feel comfortable driving on the highways. My daughter was going to be playing in a Holiday Tournament in Hawaii, so I stayed home, and Alyce and her sister took the trip.

With Mary Kate's passing, we started doing everything together. I mean everything. We determined that we should get away and have some time away from the real world. We scheduled a cruise with my wife's sister, Mary Ann, and her husband, Joe, in July.

I was having some knee problems that were affecting my mobility, so I went to my orthopedic doctor and convinced him that he should shoot me up so I could take my wife away so we could escape for a while.

He gave me some shots in my knee to keep me mobile for a while. He scheduled surgery for when we got back. We took the trip and relaxed the best we could and then went home.

Upon arrival home, I was told to report for a preexam at the hospital. I was directed to go down the hallway and go into the room on the right. I went into the room, and standing about ten feet in front of me was a nurse. She was not your normal nurse. She was dressed in an outfit that was similar to WWII, and it appeared that she was Filipino. She had a glow about her.

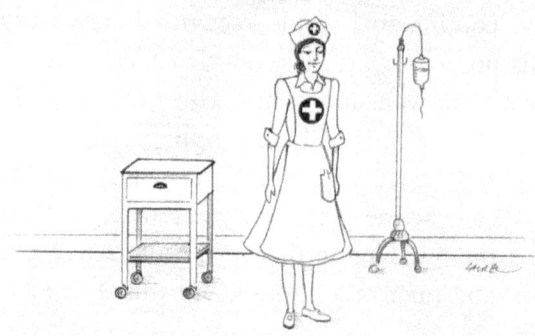

She said, "You are a Catholic, aren't you?" I responded yes while wondering what that had to do with anything. She said that I was lucky because I was about to see a doctor who sees things other doctors can't see. She explained that he was Mexican and retired but still came in for these types of exams.

Another nurse came into the room and said I was in the wrong room. I looked around, and the original nurse was gone. This nurse directed me to the correct area for the exam.

The doctor definitely looked Mexican and was short and looked fit. He marked up my knee and then asked me to stand up, which I did. He grabbed my throat and said I needed to see my doctor about my thyroid. I casually said okay, to which he responded that he was serious. So I agreed to make the appointment. Since then, I have never been able to find the first nurse again.

I had my surgery and went back to work, and then stopped in to see the plant doctor at the Chevy Plant. He was a Filipino doctor with a background in thyroid disease. He has done about a thousand thyroid removals. I asked him to check my thyroid, and he grabbed my neck and said I was okay. I also went to my personal doctor and asked him to do a hormone test on my thyroid. The results were good. I blew this off as a crazy experience.

For the next few years, I would have dreams of losing Mary Kate and not being able to find her, much like the one I had about Tommy. I believe that these types of dreams are the result of my feelings of frustration and that I couldn't prevent these tragedies from happening.

I'm very proactive by nature. I know there was nothing I could do, but when these things happen, we always ask ourselves what we could have done.

For the next few years, the moments of sorrow would come and go. Holidays and events with related memories would cause some bad moments. I found peace knowing Tommy and Kate were in a good place and that, hopefully, I would find my way back to them.

It's June of 2004, and we have scheduled a trip to Rome with my sister Cindy and her husband, Walter. Alyce and I and Cindy and Walter were married less than two weeks apart and were going to celebrate our thirtieth anniversary together in Rome.

I was having some serious back issues in June and went to see my orthopedic doctor to see what was going on. After an MRI, it was determined that I had a herniated disc in my back, and it was spread out against my sciatic nerve. The pain was significant and affected my leg and toes. I was given the option of surgery or waiting for the disc to shear off naturally. I did not choose surgery.

I was on pain pills and rehab going into September. Our trip was scheduled for mid-October, and I was in so much pain the doctor sent me to pain management for injections in my back. There were a series of three shots, spaced out over a few weeks. This was to hopefully give me some pain relief. I requested the last shot just prior to leaving for Rome.

Before leaving for the trip, I noticed I was having some short periods of rapid heart rate and shortness of breath, similar to what I would think was a panic attack. I went to see the doctor at the plant where I worked and explained the situation. He took me to the exam room and asked me to sit on the table to get my blood pressure and heart rate. As soon as I stepped up to the table, an attack started. The doctor immediately took my blood pressure and heart rate. They were off the charts. He told me to sit in the chair and take a minute.

After about two minutes, he took my heart rate and blood pressure, and everything was normal. He asked me if I was concerned about this trip at all, and I said no. He then did an EKG. He said everything looked good and that it seemed like it could have been a panic attack.

We left for Rome and, with the help of the pain pills, successfully visited the ruins and the Vatican and saw Pope John Paul II. I don't remember any attacks during that time. We completed the trip and went home.

Upon returning, I had scheduled an appointment to see my family doctor to get a PSA blood test. While walking up the long corridor to the elevators, I had another attack and had to sit down because I was getting dizzy.

After relaxing, I went to the doctor's office and told him what had happened then and prior. He checked me out and did an EKG. Both were good. He said he was going to schedule me for a stress test the next day. He told me if it gets worse, go to the emergency room.

The next day, as I entered the plant, it happened again. I almost passed out on my way to my office. I told Lynn, who works with me, to get the doctor. I also asked her to get my vehicle and drive me to the emergency room. I refused an ambulance.

Alyce met me at the emergency room. The doctor at the hospital read my vitals and asked me if I was in pain, and I said no. He scheduled a CT scan.

Alyce and I were talking in the exam room while we waited for the results. I was lying in the bed, with Alyce beside me, when the doctor came to the door, looked in, and asked where we had gone. I said Rome. He asked if we flew, and I said yes. I said we went to see the Pope. He paused a few seconds and told me I should be dead. He said that according to the test results, I should have died flying home. I said, "No...I did see the Pope."

He told me I had pulmonary embolisms. Multiple blood clots in my lungs. That resulted in a few weeks in the hospital, on my back, not moving. They further discovered two more clots in my leg. I was in no pain lying around in a hospital bed. They had no answer for why so many clots. They said I was blessed. Little did they know how true it was.

I spent a few weeks in the hospital, clearing up the clots. Before I left the hospital, they scheduled me to see an oncologist because the CT scan showed enlarged lymph nodes in my chest. I met with an oncologist from the Ireland Cancer Center (which it was called at the time) and had a discussion about my condition. He told me they thought I may have lymphoma because of the size of the lymph nodes in my chest. I asked what we do now. He suggested a PET scan to determine if there was cancer; however, it would not be covered without a cancer diagnosis. It is a test that will tell us whether there is a high level of activity based on the sugar consumption of cells in the body. Cancer lights up bright because it really likes sugar. I told him, "Let's do the scan." The scan was done, and my lymph nodes lit up like a Christmas tree. That meant I needed to have a biopsy done. The biopsy was scheduled, and the surgeon opened my neck region to enter behind my breastplate. Immediately upon doing so, he stopped and said he found the source. It appears to be thyroid cancer. Another biopsy was scheduled.

Since I wasn't moving, my back pain was quiet. However, when I got out of the hospital, my back was killing me again. In the meantime, I was trying to get surgery to shave the disc in my back to relieve the pain. No one would open me up until the cancer issue was resolved. The diagnosis was thyroid cancer, and it was advanced. Surgery was scheduled for March 5, 2005.

It's February 15, 2005, and I have been suffering with my back. Alyce and I were lying in bed, and I told her I couldn't take it anymore, I couldn't sleep, and I hurt all the time. I said I'm going to forgo the surgery and let this thing run its course. It has beaten me. Alyce started crying, and I said I'm sorry, but the back pain has taken all I've got. I prayed for help but didn't get it. Three days later, I was 100 percent pain-free. It had been so long that I almost didn't recognize the feeling of being pain-free. I told Alyce I was pain-free, and I didn't know why. I told her I would have the surgery. The surgery was done, and my thyroid was removed, along with all the lymph nodes in my neck. The surgery went well, and I was started on radiation treatments.

Around June, my back started hurting again, so I went back to my orthopedic doctor, and he did another MRI. When the results came back, he said there was both good and bad news. I said just tell me what it is. He said, "I have never seen this ever before, but your disc has pulled back in like nothing has happened, unbelievable!" He explained that the pain I was having now was mechanical and would clear up in a week. It was gone in a week, and I told Alyce, I believe God is looking after me, and I don't know why.

I've had a few more surgeries, and all but one of the lymph nodes in my chest were removed. I have been monitored twice a year ever since. It's been seventeen years, and I'm still here. I owe it to God and a number of great doctors, especially my doctor and friend Dr. Zuhayr Madhun, who has been with me through it all. I was blessed to have him guiding me through this. I thanked him for saving my life, and he responded, "God wanted you to live."

The years after my original surgery were years I would call the years of realization. During this time period, I came to recognize what had occurred and tried to determine what it all meant. In order to understand this timeframe, you need to know more about the two most important people who influenced me more deeply during this time, my wife, Alyce, and my sister Cindy. My wife, Alyce, when I met her, was a meeting that nobody could predict. During my time after my son died, there are two people who have been involved in everything medical and spiritual in my life: my wife, Alyce, and my sister Cindy. Alyce kept me stable and strong, gave me love, and brought us closer together. We shared a common pain and dealt with it relying on God and our love.

My sister Cindy was always there, even while fighting for her own life. We shared my dreams, and her prayers kept me from diving into the darkness. She unselfishly gave time to my issues while quietly isolating me from hers. She was close to God. I remember going to Virginia to see her because the doctors said they felt her time might be coming shortly. When I got there, she was in a coma, she was bloated, and her breathing was short and rapid. I felt bad because her son John wasn't there, and I knew she wanted to see him before she passed. I kissed her and whispered to her that I loved her. I returned to Cleveland.

The following day, I received a phone call saying that she was up in her bed playing her guitar. It was unbelievable! The next thing I knew, she was out of the hospital and, yes, driving. I believe she had some unfinished business. She had moved in with her daughter Jackie and her family. She had a hospital bed and was cherishing her grandchildren. Alyce and I went to visit her, and I also went to a Steeler/Redskins football game with Walter. She talked to me, and we drank a beer together. I never saw her drink a beer except once with me in New Zealand after her daughter Jackie's wedding. It was a good moment.

We said our final goodbyes and left in the morning. I told her I loved her and asked if we were okay. She said she loved me, and we were okay. Her son came and saw her, which was priority 1 for her at that time. A couple of days later, she passed. This was another tough issue for me. I only remember crying four times in my life: crying seeing my dad after my parents separated, then getting the Christmas wreath after Tommy died, then when Mary Kate died, and lastly, when Cindy died. I had whimpered at times but rarely ever really cried. I've learned that crying is not a bad thing and is therapeutic when tied to grief.

About a year after she passed, I had another dream, a special dream. I saw Cindy teaching students in a small horseshoe-shaped auditorium with a chalkboard beside her. She was standing and writing some numbers on the board. I was watching from out of sight at the top of the auditorium. I hadn't shown myself to her when she looked up at me and sternly said, "You know what you need to do, these are the numbers." The numbers she wrote on the board were displayed with 1014 on top and 2022 underneath it. I had no idea what they meant! My original reaction was to do what the members of my family would do. I played them in the lottery Pick 4 game. Well, that didn't go well. I spent the money for a month and nothing! My family fairly often won money based on dreams. It bothered me because I felt it was something important. For some reason, it bothered me for the next seven years; however, I never did anything about it and never had another dream about her.

Years later, at a dinner party in 2016, I told everybody that my dad, his brothers, and my grandfather all died at seventy-one. My cousin made the comment that we men in the family are going to go at seventy-one. Alyce didn't like it, and I asked, "When will I be seventy-one?" It's 10/12/2022. At that exact moment, I realized Cindy's numbers represented a date. A date for what, I don't know. Some people might say, "How could you not know it was a date?" Well, it was 2009 when she wrote it, and I never related it to a date because in 2009, 2020 and 1014 just looked like other numbers. I still don't know what it means, good or bad, but I believe it will be relevant. Since the dream of my sister Cindy, I have had no other dreams of a spiritual nature. The date 10/14/2022 came, and I spent it with my dear friend Mr. Fong, with whom I have had many spiritual and world-saving discussions. The day came and went, and no recognizable events occurred that I would attribute to this dream. Maybe it will have some relevance when I look back in the future. Unlike my other dreams, this one was not associated with God. It is my understanding that God is not fond of people seeking counsel or visions from the dead.

Well, not a dream, but in December of 2009, I had a wonderful experience that for me was a spiritual happening. I received a call from my son-in-law saying that people were always asking Alecia when they were going to have children. He said they had been trying for four years, even seeking assistance from the Cleveland Clinic. When people asked her when she was going to have children, she would cry. He asked me if Alyce and I could put out the word not to say anything. I said fine, just put her on the phone. I asked her if she wanted a child, and she said yes. I told her I could help her. She asked me what I meant by that. I said, "I will pray the Rosary for you." I told her when I pray the Rosary, I pray for others, not myself, and I have never been let down. She doubtingly said okay. I started praying, and Alyce told her sister Kathleen, and the next thing I knew, almost every prayer group was praying for her. Alyce contacted her best friend in Spain, and the next thing you know, people all over

Spain were praying. It just started to grow. In January, she told us she was pregnant but not to say anything till she was at least three months along. In my eyes, my grandson was a blessing from God. It wasn't just my prayers but the prayers of many. I know some people don't believe in prayers; that's their belief, and they have a right to feel that way, but I believe the future for them may be very difficult.

This is my story. It is true. When these things happened, I was very open about what I call spiritual events when they occurred. I was particularly open with my sister Cindy, my wife, Alyce, and some close friends. They knew something out of the ordinary was happening.

CHAPTER 12

Just When You Think It's Done!

It's November of 2023, and I have been working on this book for a number of years and thought I had it complete. Apparently, I assumed wrong. It seems every time I thought I was getting close, something would happen to cause me to question whether or not I was doing the right thing by writing this book. Well, as fate would have it, I had another lifesaving event to add to the series of special treatments God has provided me.

It was October 12, my seventy-second birthday. I was thinking about how I would say that we Danzey men don't make it past seventy-one. I was having a nice day, and Alyce made me a special meal. I eat early because I limit my eating hours to between 12:00 p.m. and 4:00 p.m.

That evening, I felt like I had really eaten too much, even to the extent of being stuffed. I actually hadn't eaten much at all, and I couldn't understand how I felt this way.

That night, I started throwing up blood. However, I didn't realize it was blood because it was all black. I thought I had food poisoning. My wife insisted I go to the emergency room at the hospital.

I couldn't walk because I thought I would pass out, so I went in sitting in a wheelchair. I got registered and then had to wait about eight hours in the waiting room. When I got to go in, my blood pressure crashed, and they admitted me, but they had no rooms. I spent the next thirty-six hours waiting for a bed.

I told them at 4:00 a.m. that I was leaving and to bring me the discharge papers. I couldn't sleep because it was so noisy, and I couldn't even get assistance, so I wet myself.

I called my wife and told her to come get me. She was not happy, and my daughter told her not to let me leave the hospital.

I was waiting in the waiting room for her. She showed up and told me she did not want me to leave. I asked her to wheel me to the bathroom, and I had her wait by the door, just in case something would happen. I had another bad experience at that time, so I agreed not to leave.

She informed the desk, and they told her I would be placed back on the current wait list and that I could expect an eleven-hour wait, and wait I did.

Once inside, everything went better. I was placed in a room and was well taken care of. A gastro team was called in, I was put under, and a procedure was performed.

When I woke up, the doctor's team came in and said that my wife had saved my life. He said that if she would have let me go home, I would have died.

My God had intervened in spite of my arrogance and used my wife and daughter to save my life. It was not my time to pass, and God had more planned for me. Maybe he wants this book finished.

CHAPTER 13

Why Now?

When you experience so many significant emotional events and occasions of spiritual assistance, you wonder, *Why me?* Further, you want to know, *What am I supposed to do with this experience?*

In my deeper moments, I would talk about it and sometimes to people I didn't even know. Obviously, it has been weighing on me.

Upon hearing my stories, people, mostly women, would tear up. Some would cry and hug me. Apparently, they were feeling my sorrow, but that was not my intention.

I felt a need to talk about my experience, and at the same time, it gave me moments of relief knowing other people could understand how deeply emotional these events had been for me.

In 2018, I was emotionally exhausted, and I decided I needed to start taking care of myself and found a physical trainer to help me regain my physical health. I found a trainer who pushed me hard. Her name was Pam Houston.

She transformed me physically but also became a friend. She had heard my story and pushed me to write a book. She felt it was the kind of story that may help others. I believe that she was one of those perchance connections that was meant to guide me in that direction.

I have been working on this book for several years. At times, it became so emotionally draining that I would put it down for months. It seemed to me that this book would be written when it was meant to be written.

It's now 2024, and I believe that the time has come.

Our world is becoming belligerent to those with strong Christian beliefs. When I say Christian beliefs, I mean the religion, not necessarily the church. I believe the church is run by people who operate like governments.

Governments seem to become corrupt and alter the meanings of laws to meet their agendas. The religious churches seem to alter the meaning of the Bible and church laws to meet their agenda. I don't want this to be totally inclusive because there are always some that get it right in spite of the others. Hold on to your religious beliefs dearly.

I believe we are all tied to an infinite web of connections that fall under God's plan. We all have a destiny that is a part of God's plan. We cannot determine our destiny; however, free will may knock us off course, but there is always a connection that brings us back to where we belong.

Our destiny is not always pretty or easy, but it has a purpose that only God knows. I believe all people are God's people, and no person knows what someone else's destiny is and how it affects God's plan. Those who don't believe in destiny yet call themselves Christians, remember this, the Bible covers mankind's destiny from the beginning to "everlasting" life.

I believe that's why God judges the living and the dead. It's not man's job. We live in a world where people judge others as being different and against God's law. I say let God judge them, for only he can pass such judgment. Mankind cannot judge fairly because we don't have the knowledge that God has.

This opinion of mine was influenced by a movie called *The Shack*. This movie was based on William Paul Young's novel *The Shack*. The movie, as I see it, addresses why God is the judge. God has so many more data points to make a judgment. However, man's judgment might not be the same as God's.

We tend to judge people with our beliefs, assumptions, and our eyes. What we believe isn't always correct. What we assume more often than not, is not verified. What we see with our eyes isn't always real. Sometimes people aren't always as bad as we think nor are they as good as we think they are.

I think most of our problems are the result of us thinking we know how God thinks, which is impossible to know. My boss at work would always want to make sure he had enough data points to make a good decision. God has an infinite number of data points.

My point is that we allow others to develop what is called groupthink by controlling data points, some of which may be true and some not. The purpose is to control what the masses believe, thus assisting in supporting a particular agenda. If you can change what people believe by simply studying human nature and understanding how they make decisions, you can make them believe anything. Groupthink is dangerous. God gave us the ability to think for ourselves and not surrender it to those with bad agendas.

I have given you my story. It is a true story, and you can take from it what you want. I am not trying to force any beliefs on you; I am only telling you what happened. I will give you my feelings about how I perceive the things that happened.

CHAPTER 14

My Perception

All my life, I felt that things happened the way they were supposed to happen. Sometimes bad things happen to you, or you do bad things to others. When bad things happen to you, maybe they happen to help someone else recognize how bad it was and that they need to change their ways.

When you do something bad to others, you learn you need to change your ways and correct your behavior, knowing that there is a price for your actions. There is always a price you pay. God wouldn't have sent Jesus to the cross if there wasn't a price to pay for sins.

As far as my life goes, I have done emotional damage to others and, at times, even serious emotional damage. I know there is emotional pain to pay for my actions if that process has not already started.

It's funny, but someone said that the more you get to know God, the more you realize how much you have sinned. I have come to the realization that my life has been a continuous run of sins.

I'll lie in bed some nights thinking, and then I just remember another sin or sins I committed. Sin is sin, and you cannot go back in time and change it; you just have to remember there will be a price to pay, but in the eyes of God, it will be forgiven. Some people believe that by accepting Jesus, your sins are forgiven. I believe that, but the forgiveness may come with a price. You accept that price, knowing you have received forgiveness from God.

I laugh when people say they will accept Jesus at the end of their earthly life, and all will be good. I don't think so. There are a lot of people out there in the churches, media, and governments supplying false understandings of how God works. Only God knows how God works.

As I write, you see me say what I believe and not what God believes. God has given us guidelines to live by and given us the avenue to be forgiven. The word *forgiven* is a big word in the religious world.

I think of movies where a person is being put to death in the infamous electric chair, and the family of the victim says, "I forgive you." That doesn't mean it's all right. Don't throw the switch.

I'm only thinking as a person, not God, but I believe God never promised there would be no consequences for your sins. Learn from your mistakes and change your behavior, and your path to eternal life will be easier. Consequences for your actions may be dealt with while on earth or when you meet God.

I want to give you my perception of my life and how it has played out through my eyes.

There will be those people who will ask the question of why God was so concerned about me. Those people know I am far from being a saint. I have three things to respond to this concern. First, Jesus preaches to the unbelievers and sinners. He already doesn't have to preach to the believers; they are already in his camp. Second, some of Jesus's closest believers were at some point not looked upon so favorably by most people. Paul was a murderer. He sought out Christians and had them imprisoned and some killed. Mary Magdalene was a prostitute, and Matthew was a tax collector. The point is that God uses the misfits and the saints to do his work.

I find the word *misfits* so attractive for this narrative because I heard it used on SkyWatch TV, and I believe they used it to describe how God uses those people to push forward his message because of their situations. I personally like the term because it describes me.

Thirdly, "I don't know!"

My last twenty years have been blessed by prayers. Maybe God is answering the prayers of those who have been praying for me.

Maybe they are the important ones and it's not about me. I believe God is trying to bring me home. There is a reason why I'm still alive.

I do not know what destiny God has laid out for me; it could be good or bad, but whatever it is, I accept it. Others will say the things that happened are just things of chance or creations of my mind. My mind isn't capable of showing me the future or altering my damaged body parts or preventing my death.

Looking back, I was shown in a dream the signs of what was to come. The priest blessing the throats told me that there is something going to happen, and it concerns the throat. Four years later, I was diagnosed with advanced thyroid cancer. I was shown my sweet Mary Kate next to Jesus. My sister Cindy was also there with Jesus. My son was there also.

I didn't know that I was being blessed with this insight. I honestly didn't know how much was being shown to me until Mary Kate passed, and I realized that God wanted me to understand that he is there, and he knows what's happening. Not everybody can say they were informed ahead of time that their child would die.

At this point, I became a knower and not just a believer. The final piece of my first dream with Jesus, I believe, was a reminder that he always knew what was going on.

This will be hard for some to believe, and I can understand it. Being an open book, I promise many people knew of my dreams well before things started to reveal themselves. Some people probably believed at that time that they were the product of a broken heart. That may be true, but Jesus was the producer of these visions.

I'm not sure that I will be around to understand my destiny; however, I'm sure there will be those that try to track it to determine what it was. Remember this, the connections are unlimited, and only God knows the answer.

What I have learned from these events in my life is that Jesus is real, we are all connected, and death is not an ending but another beginning.

ACKNOWLEDGMENTS

Nothing is accomplished in life without the helping hands of others.

To the entire Martin and Nedra Delaney clan and their husbands, wives, and children. Without them, there would be no story. God bless them all.

To my entire family, my mother and father and sisters, including my sister's families. Family makes us who we are.

Special thanks to the following:

To artist Laurel Herbold for the beautiful illustrations for my story.

To Dr. Zuhayr T. Madhun for the twenty-four years of keeping me alive. I consider him my doctor and my friend.

To Elise Delong, my sister-in-law, for her thoughts and ideas.

To Doug Bardwell, my brother-in law, for his editing and technology assistance.

To Joe and Mary Ann Demay for all their kindness in helping Alyce and me to keep our mental health through these years.

To Oksana, Lynn, and Diane, thanks for helping keeping me together at work through these trying times. Love you, ladies.

A big thank you to William Marsh and Rose Gerchak for their prayers for the last twenty-four years. Maybe I am alive because God is answering your prayers.

Thank you to my daughter, Alecia, and her husband, Chad, for our two grandchildren that filled the empty space left in our hearts.

Most of all, thanks to God Almighty for staying with me through everything.

ABOUT THE AUTHOR

My name is Thomas Livingston Danzey III. I graduated from Penn Hills HS in 1969. Started college in 1969 at Auburn University. In 1972, I joined the US Navy. Honorably discharged in 1974. Married Alyce Delaney in 1974. Graduated from Auburn University in 1977. I started work with General Motors in 1978. Had three children, Thomas IV, Alecia, and Mary Kate. Retired from General Motors in October 2016. Most of my career at General Motors was spent as the supervisor of labor relations but also held positions of supervisor of safety and supervisor of salary personnel. Love God, family, and USA.

Printed in the USA
CPSIA information can be obtained
at www.ICGtesting.com
CBHW031924220924
14685CB00025B/502